SHIPPING CONTAINER HOMES

Build Amazing DIY Shipping Container Home Step by Step with no Experience For Debt-Free Living

William Watson

Shipping Container Homes

Copyright © 2013 by William Watson.

This book is a work of fiction. Names, characters, businesses, organiza- tions, places, events and incidents either are the product of the author's imagination or are used fictitiously. Any resemblance to actual persons, living or dead, events, or locales is entirely coincidental.

First Edition: June 2021

C O N T E N T S

INTRODUCTION

Container homes are simply what they sound like: homes constructed from steel shipping containers that you see on trucks, trains, and ships transporting goods all over the world. People are constructing homes of all shapes and sizes out of these massive Lego blocks.

Shipping containers are generally available in 10ft, 20ft, and 40ft. The smallest shipping container may provide around 100 square feet of floor space for a shipping container home. Eight larger containers can be combined to form a two-story house with a floor area of around 1400 square feet. Hundreds of container micro-apartments can be combined to form a large apartment building.

What are the advantages of using shipping containers to build apartments, studios, offices, and cabins? There are about 14 million 'out-of-service' containers in the country, so there are plenty to go around. And there's something about giant blocks that appeals to me!

Aside from being trendy, interest in container homes is part of a broader movement toward prefabricated and modular homes as a way to save money. A lot of potential homeowners want to save money on building and maintenance. There's also a perception that container homes help with recycling.

What is a shipping container house?

A shipping container house is any structure built out of a shipping container, but the resulting structures can be varied. Shipping containers are usually 20 feet by 8 feet or 40 feet by 8 feet in size. The smaller container provides approximately 160 square feet of living space, while the larger container provides 320 square feet. There are two height choices: standard (8.5 feet high) or high cube (approximately a foot of additional vertical living space). Some shipping container homes stop here, converting the small spaces into tiny homes or offices.

However, many builders and homeowners, including this one in Missouri, combine containers to make larger houses. Walls are often demolished to build more spacious interiors in homes with many containers, and conventional building techniques add exterior materials and additional rooms.

Some containers can be stacked to create multi-level homes, while others can be twisted and turned Jenga-style to create stunning architectural masterpieces.

The Advantages of Shipping Container Homes

1. Prefab Shipping Container Homes

Many shipping container homes are available as prefabricated modular homes, making construction time shorter. Some organizations advertise delivery in as little as ten weeks! The majority of building code inspections are completed at the factory, which simplifies and expedites the process. If you're building a do-it-yourself project or designing a custom home, the container provides a pleasant pre-built framework to work with.

2. Ease of Transport and Finding a Site

Moving containers around the world are possible thanks to a global infrastructure. Once they arrive at your place, they are reasonably easy to install on a prepared foundation.

3. Shipping Container Homes Have Predictable Costs

The majority of the job is completed on a factory floor for a fixed price. The only variable costs are delivery to the site, foundation, site preparation, assembly, and utility connections. Container houses, on the other hand, are not necessarily less costly. Estimates differ, and some say you'll save 5-10%, depending on what you're comparing to.

4. Recycled Shipping Container Homes

The environmental appeal of a container home stems from the fact that you are repurposing a shipping industry byproduct to create a home. This can be beneficial, but as we can see, it is not always the case or the best option. Some of the benefits, such as speed of construction and predictable pricing, apply to all prefabricated and modular houses, not just those built with shipping containers. Container homes, on the other hand, benefit from the global infrastructure designed to transport shipping containers. Also, critics agree that container homes can be useful in situations where local building expertise is lacking or where emergency shelters need to be transported quickly. The flexibility of container transportation is a major benefit in these scenarios. Container homes are often advertised as environmentally friendly because they are claimed to be constructed from recycled containers, thereby conserving metal resources. There are a lot of old shipping containers out there that are no longer in use, and converting them into homes has a lot of appeals. But, in terms of sustainability, is a container home the best use of a container? Many people would disagree.

Disadvantages of Shipping Container Homes

1. Shipping Container Homes Are Not Always Effective Recycling

Most factory-built container homes are made from 'one-use' containers that have only been used once. These containers are usually in good condition, with no dents or rust, and are thus better for building with than containers that have been deemed "out-of-service" and may have been damaged over time. Taking a box with a long shipping life out of service after a single use is not effective recycling. And a container contains much more steel than is needed to construct a house; if recycled as steel, it could provide enough steel studs for 14 framed houses of the same size.

2. Shipping Container Homes Could Have Structural Issues

The corners of a shipping container are very strong, but the roof isn't, so you'll usually need to build another roof over it, particularly if there will be snow. The corrugated steel walls are also crucial to the structure's resilience. This means that every time a wide window or door opening is cut out, new reinforcement is needed. When they're stacked to make bigger houses, welded (expensive) reinforcement is needed anywhere two containers meet in a non-corner spot. Any future renovations will require extensive engineering and welding.

3. Are Shipping Container Homes Safe?

It's always impossible to tell what was shipped in a used container – anything from common household items to dangerous industrial products – or what it's been through. Since the paints and finishes used on containers are industrial and designed for shipping across the ocean rather than for residential use, they can contain lead and toxic pesticides.

What Is The Standard Size of a Shipping Container Home?
The size of shipping containers is limited, and plumbing, HVAC, insulation, and other systems will quickly consume them. Since a container was made to fit on a train, it's narrow, and regular furniture won't fit. A typical container is also just 8 feet wide and 8 feet 6 inches tall, leaving little headroom after insulation and wiring.

How Do You Insulate a Shipping Container Home?
The narrow shape of a shipping container makes it difficult to properly insulate the exterior. A relatively thin layer of insulation with a high R-value per inch, such as polyurethane spray foam, is mostly used to avoid taking up interior space. While spray foam is an efficient and airtight insulator, the blowing agents used in many brands of spray foam are powerful greenhouse gases.

Costs Of Shipping Containers Homes
So what will a shipping container home cost? Container homes that are smaller and more basic will cost between

$10,000 to $35,000. Large homes with multiple shipping containers and amenities will cost between $100,000 and $175,000 to build. In certain cases, shipping container homes are half the price per square foot of conventional stick-built homes. However, comparing apples to apples is difficult, as there are several variables to consider.

So what can increase the cost? Although land costs and climate requirements are important factors, other factors to consider include:

• Size, design, layout, and the number of containers required
• Cleaning cost if the container is used
• Welding and Fabrication requirements
• Plumbing and electrical
• Kitchen and bathroom finishes
• Lofts
• Siding
• Flooring
• Windows
• Insulation
• Doors
• and more.

There is a report of a basic shipping container home built by an engineer in Canada for only $20,000. A pre-fabricated container house, on the other hand, has a price tag that is comparable to that of a normal home.

How Long Does A Shipping Container Home Last?

Shipping container homes should last at least 25 years, but they can last much longer if they are well-maintained or have siding on the outside. The most common problem that can shorten the life of a shipping container home is rust. It's important to check and search for rust spots in your shipping container house. To prevent rust from spreading, any problem areas should be treated and fixed.

Why shipping containers homes?

Like other new products, the shipping container was designed to solve a problem: how to move goods efficiently and safely through land and sea. Of course, humans had been doing so for thousands of years, but in inefficient ways most of the time. The crucial innovation of containers was that they were:

- Large enough to carry thousands of cubic feet of merchandise while still being small enough to fit on a truck and travel on regular roads.
- Uniform enough that any truck or ship could carry any container, but versatile enough that they could be used for dry goods, refrigerated goods, bulk liquids, and so on.
- Strong enough to withstand an often perilous voyage at sea, but light enough to be moved with cranes, forklifts, and other material handling equipment

The planet has been changed by the economic transport of goods from distant countries, thanks to the work of people like Malcolm McLean, in just a few short decades. Steel shipping containers were a key component in making it possible. Consider how convenient it would be if you could fly anywhere in the world and use the same type of plug or make transactions in the same currency. It's difficult to achieve this degree of global standardization, but that's exactly what shipping containers have done!

One element McLean could not have anticipated was the gradual accumulation of surplus containers as a result of trade imbalances. In the 1980s, this and other factors prompted pioneers to investigate converting shipping containers into usable structures. We now have thousands of examples of amazing container structures thanks to the imagination of both talented designers and ordinary people like you.

Chapter 1: LAWS AND PERMITS

If you're interested in shipping container homes, it's a good idea to look into the local container home laws and regulations in your area.

This is the safest way to ensure that you would not breach any regulations if you start building a home out of shipping containers. The guidelines presented below are intended to provide you with valuable information and shed light on this situation.

Although shipping containers were designed with a specific function in mind, that is to transport large quantities of products around the world, many people found their incredible potential for repurposing.

It's easy to see why some people considered using them for home construction because they were engineered to be sturdy and durable, with a capacity of up to 55,000 lbs.

The demand for shipping container houses grew as a result of the concept of recycling and repurposing large metal containers, of having a new and unique-looking home, and of the flexibility promised by this solution. In today's world, the construction industry alone is worth many billions of dollars. However, without the necessary permits, shipping containers cannot be used to build a house. Permits cannot be obtained until the containers have been licensed by the regulatory bodies in charge of this region.

Who are the regulatory bodies that have the authority to grant the required approvals? The conversion of shipping containers into units suitable for human habitation is governed by the International Residential Code and the International Building Code. The International Code Council was the first organization to provide an official guideline for using shipping containers in commercial and residential construction. This guideline was issued in February 2016 and it is called ICC-ES AC462. The Modular Building Institute and the National Portable Storage Association are likely to influence future regulations. Even then, the majority of the regulations in this field are provided by local building code bodies, so it's worth checking them out.

What Kind of Permits Do I Need for Shipping Container House?
Everything starts with a design, just like every other construction project. Ideally, you can enlist the assistance of a skilled designer who can create the perfect design for your shipping container home while taking into account the environment in which you reside. Still, it's best not to proceed to anything complex or spend too much money before you speak with a representative from the local municipalities.

Since local regulations can vary from those issued by the state, it's best to figure this out before you start spending consistent amounts of money on your dream. Presenting a skilled design to the building commissioner, on the other hand, would show that you are determined and committed to uphold the requirements and construct a reliable home from the onset.

You will be asked to show a paper containing the technical requirements as well as a technical drawing of the containers you are about to use. This is typically required so that authorities can determine if the containers are appropriate for use as a residential structure. If this is a necessity, obtaining all of this information can be difficult because you would need to find the manufacturer of the container, which is, in most cases, located in China.

Since shipping containers are typically leased to a variety of companies throughout their lives, you'll have to work your way down the line before you reach the container's provider. If you're fortunate, the supplier or manufacturer will be able to provide you with a specification sheet as well as a professional drawing.

Finally, you'll need permission from your local authorities. Despite the fact that shipping container homes are not a new concept, many areas are still unfamiliar with such requests and may not know how to handle your permit application. While finding the person who is issuing the permit can be difficult, it is always a good idea to start by speaking with the person in charge of building permits in your area. A building permit isn't always required, so if that's the case for you, skip this section and get to work on your shipping container house.

Container Home Laws – Is it Legal to Build Shipping Container Home in My state?

A shipping container home could be one of the most cost-effective ways for many Americans to finally have the home of their dreams. But, before you put this on your wish list, make sure it's legal to build a home like this in your state. As a result, the issue of whether or not building a shipping container home is legal in your state arises.

The answer to this question is that most states in the U.S allow the building of homes out of shipping containers. Many of those who don't allow it yet are considering it and also looking for ways to regulate it properly.

Bear in mind that even if your state permits the building of shipping container homes, your city may not. So, once again, check your local laws on this issue. To learn about the legal terms in your state, you'll need to contact the county or city planner to check their recommendations in this situation. Even if you get permission from the planner to construct a shipping container house, you must also adhere to local zoning and building codes.

What are Shipping Container Building Codes?

Aside from zoning, you'll need to be aware of building codes. This is critical because a code would tell you what criteria should be followed when constructing something in a specific region. As a result, you won't be able to construct a structure that does not comply with the building code in the region where you intend to build it.

One of the things you must prove when applying for a building permit is that you can follow the building code in the area where you intend to build your shipping container house. You will only be able to get the approval you need if you can show that you will comply.

These building codes are generally issued by the International Residential Code and the International Building Code in the United States. They can also change once a year or twice a year, so it's worth double-checking these codes before you begin your construction project. Building codes are one of the first things you should review before coming up with a design for your shipping container home since certain states have their codes in this sector.

Can I Apply Online for Permits?

Yes, you can apply for a permit online if you know the department to submit your application to and if you have all of the necessary documents. This is why speaking with someone from the municipality could be beneficial.

You'll learn more about the local laws governing shipping container homes, as well as what you'll need to get started building one. You can start collecting permits, finish your home's design, and everything else required to apply for a permit online once you have all of the details you need. Obtaining a permit, regardless of its intent, is a time-consuming and patient process. Fortunately, you may obtain the permit you want online. By accessing online permits you can apply for the permit you need conveniently and comfortably. However, double-check that you have everything you'll need to submit a qualified permit. This means you should already have all of the required approvals from your local legislation.

What is Shipping Container Zoning

Every state in the United States has its zoning regulations governing the areas available for building purposes. The zoning would specify the types of structures that can be constructed in a given location. The zones are designed to aid a city's development in a harmonious manner and accordance with the municipality's plans. Huston, for example, is an exception to this law since it does not have zoning. As a result, you should review the zoning code of the area where you want to build your shipping container home before getting started. The zoning code will tell you what types of structures are permitted in the region, so you can plan your future home accordingly.

Chapter 2: BUYING THE CONTAINERS

Tips You Need To Know Before Building A Shipping Container Home

One of the niche trends in sustainable design of the past few years has been the re-use of shipping containers to create the structure of a building. Shipping containers are well-suited for use in houses due to their compact size, and their appeal stems from their obvious simplicity: you get a room shipped in one piece, and you can stack them together to make multiple rooms or tie them together make larger rooms.

But, of course, nothing is ever as simple as it seems, and using shipping containers to build a home is still fraught with difficulties - particularly since the concept is still relatively new, and few people have the experience needed to construct one without a hitch. That's why we have enlisted the help of 23 experts from around the world - designers and owners who have faced obstacles to create their own container homes - to find out what they wish they had learned before taking on the project. Check out their 11 top tips.

1. Examine the containers you're purchasing " "I wish I hadn't bought my containers without seeing them first; I trusted the company's word that they would be in good condition. They were all beaten to a pulp."

2. Invest a little more in a one-trip container.
"I wish I had known that a One-Trip container isn't that expensive and is like brand new."

3. Familiarize yourself with the local rules in your area.

"Every country has its set of rules and regulations. This means that a container house in the United States is not the same as a container house in Denmark. That is something that most people do not consider. Although the container is a generic commodity, environment, fire regulations, and other factors are not..."

4. Find A Contractor That Can Do It All

"The one thing we would have done better is to find a single contractor to assist us in the process rather than hiring one for obtaining and changing the containers and another for finishing out the interior."

5. Understand the Shipping Container Market

"I wish I knew there were containers that are taller than 8 feet."

- Mark Wellen, Rhotenberry Wellen Architects

6. Understand The Shipping Container's Structure

"I think it's crucial to consider how their structural integrity works—for example, the two long walls are both load-bearing and bracing, so if you cut a hole in one, you'd have to compensate."

7. Don't Expect To Make A Huge Saving

"What I wish I had known that building a house out of shipping containers cost about the same as building a house out of sticks."

8. Minimize The Required Welding

"Welding takes a long time and is costly, so try to avoid it as much as possible."

9. Know How To Insulate

"I wish I had known how to insulate a shipping container; we ended up soldering elements on the walls and then spraying them with anti-fire foam insulation."

"We wish we'd known that in cold countries, you must ensure

that you have enough insulation to avoid condensation."

10. Plan Ahead For Plumbing

"Having all of the plumbing chases cut out of the container floors and ceilings to conveniently run pipe until they were stacked would have made a significant difference."

11. Have A Strategy To Cope With Wind

"We weren't expecting too much wind on-site, and we're now having to block it out with vegetation because the container makes a lot of noise when there are strong winds."

PLANNING

How To Plan Your Shipping Container Home

Planning is essential for any project, and shipping container homes are no exception.

The typical new home project goes over budget and time by around 20 percent. You must create and adhere to a solid plan.

Let's take a closer look at how to schedule the design of your shipping container home correctly.

Set Your Budget

Setting a budget is the first step in building a house.

It's pointless to decide to create a 4,000-square-foot house if you only have $50,000 to work with.

Determine how much money you have in your account. If you can borrow money from a bank or a family member, the amount would be added to the total amount of money you have available for the project. This is your budget.

Have a 20% contingency fund. A contingency fund is a set of funds set aside to cover unforeseen costs that might arise during the construction of your house. The majority of construction projects have unforeseen costs.

With total cash available of $150,000, this is how the contingency fund is measured. 20% of $150,000 = $30,000.

Subtract the $30,000 contingency sum from your total available funds amount of $150,000. This leaves you with the actual budget for building your container house. Your construction budget is now $120,000, plus a $30,000 contingency budget. Your project must be focused on that $120,000 amount, with $30,000 set aside for any problems that might occur.

Decide and Finalize Your Design

It's now time to start planning your shipping container house. By the way, you can figure out your budget before moving on to this stage so that you can prepare realistically.

You can design anything, from a single container tiny house to a multi-story mansion! The possibilities for shipping container combinations are virtually infinite, and they can be tailored to your exact specifications.

The best way to plan is to start with the logical questions before getting bogged down in the details, such as how many containers do I need, how do I insulate my house, and so on.

Instead, consider things like what the building will be used for, how many people will use it, and so on. Take it one step at a time. Make the most important decisions first. Then, as you go along, add more info. Keep in mind that the more precise your responses, the better your design will be.

Changing your mind about a design halfway through construction costs a lot of money. Don't make the same mistake as the couple who wanted to remove a container's internal wall. They then decided they didn't want the open-plan room after all and reinstalled the wall. They lost $5,000 in material and time as a result of the changes.

This cost could have been avoided with better planning!

Decide Who Will Build It

Once you've settled on a concept for your shipping container home, you'll need to consider who will build it.

Many people choose to make their shipping container

structures. This is a more cost-effective and rewarding option. If you want to construct a shipping container home yourself, consider if you have sufficiently appropriate experience and practical skills.

If you don't have the necessary skills or time, you should consider hiring a contractor to build your home for you. Contractors are usually more experienced and can complete the project in less time. They would, however, be costly. If you're considering hiring a contractor, ensure you:

- Ask for references.
- Do they guarantee their work?
- How long does the guarantee last?
- Do they have liability insurance?

Where Will You Build Your Shipping Container Home?

You've agreed on a budget, a design for your container house, and who will build it. It's now time to look for a piece of land that suits your needs.

I advise people to design their container home before they look for land so that they can design the exact shipping container home they want rather than one that is limited by a specific piece of land.

Determine a specific area where you want to develop before looking for a plot of land. You can search for land online using sites like Zillow, or you can do it the old fashioned way by driving around. You can sometimes get an absolute bargain! Don't undervalue the importance of driving around the place you've chosen. Look for any signs that say "for sale." Speak with the people who live there. Locals may be aware of land that will be available for purchase before it appears on the real estate market.

Once you've found a piece of land that you like, make an

appointment to meet with the local zoning/planning department. You must speak with them to determine whether or not they are willing to issue you a building permit to construct a shipping container home in their jurisdiction. If the local planning department is adamantly opposed to the idea at this point, it may be better to find a plot of land in a different district.

Is Your Shipping Container Home Feasible?

Do you have the necessary skills and tools to build a shipping container home? Building a shipping container home is time-consuming and expensive, and it necessitates a wide range of skills.

Time and money are the two most valuable resources you would need. Then you'll need either the DIY know-how and ability to turn the shipping container into a home, or the financial means to employ someone to do it for you.

Before you begin construction, you should think about where you would get your building materials. For example, if you want to construct a shipping container home but live 1,000 miles away from the nearest container depot, it will not be feasible. Getting your containers shipped over such a distance will cost you a lot of money and take a long time.

Building permits/planning approval is the last important factor to consider. It's a sad fact, but you won't be able to get a building permit to build a shipping container home in certain parts of the world. If this is the stance of your local planning department, then you'll have a hard time persuading them to change their minds

It's often easier to decide to construct a container home in a different district with different zoning and planning regulations!

You should now be able to plan your new shipping container home, from budgeting to finding a plot of land.

Chapter 3: SITE PREPARATION

Before you send your containers to the building site, there is a surprising amount of site work to be done. If you don't think about and execute these things early in the project, you'll end up with a lot of costly rework later.

At a high level, the site planning and preparation you do now is meant to ensure that the land is ready for the building site, the building site is ready for the containers, and the containers are ready for your container home design and lifestyle. It's an essential part of the overall project planning for your container homebuilding.

Many of the factors mentioned below interact with one another; changing one affects many others. In container home planning, finding the right balance between conflicting interests is a common theme, and this process is no exception.

Deciding on Location

Before you (or anyone else) begins actual work on your house, you must first determine where you want your container home to be mounted. There are a lot of things to think about, and some of them might already be on your mind subconsciously.

We think that having them written down allows you to be transparent and honest about the factors that influence your decision.

Sun and Shade

The sun may be both a blessing and a curse depending on

your climate. It can warm you up on a chilly morning, but it can also cause you to become blind when drinking your morning coffee.

It can give your interior spaces a gentle, natural glow, but it can also induce solar thermal gain, which necessitates the use of more air conditioning.

Pay attention to how the sun interacts with and region on your property at various times of the day when you start to narrow down the possible building sites on your property. Shade from nearby trees and bushes is important, but you can also be influenced by things like water reflections and how topography affects horizon elevation. Remember that when deciduous trees lose their leaves in the fall and winter, the shade will be diminished.

You should also consider how the sun acts at various times of the year. In different seasons, the sun moves across the sky in a different trajectory depending on the latitude.

SunCalc is an excellent tool for calculating the altitude of the sun over the horizon (in degrees) for every location on the globe at any time and date. It can also assist you in considering roof overhangs for doors and windows that protect from the hot summer sun while allowing in the warm winter sun.

Topography and Drainage

Topography and drainage, which are closely related, also need your attention. The form of the land is referred to as topography, and the way water flows through it is referred to as drainage. When assessing project locations, you must consider not only how it would be to live there, but also how it would be to build there.

Container homes usually do not need a slab foundation, which is one of their benefits. Because of their inherent strength, they can normally be supported only at their four corners and 'bridge over' any terrain changes if a level foundation system can be designed and installed underneath them. However, if access to building the foundation is restricted, this last step may be costly.

Topography has a strong influence on water and drainage. While having easy access to a pond or stream can sound appealing, consider the risk of flooding and how high the water may rise.

You may also have seasonal pools that form in low spots on the land, as well as seasonal erosion that happens during heavy rains and threatens your foundation. Observing the property during a rainstorm will help you understand how water flows through it and what steps you may need to take to divert or contain it.

Water may also be a haven for insects such as mosquitos, harmful animals such as snakes, and noisy birds. So, once again, we suggest spending time exploring the land to learn how these factors can affect you.

Views

The view out, or what they see outside through the different windows and doors, is what most people think about when they think of their container home's view. A view of a valley, a distant mountain peak, a peaceful stream, or the city skyline can all add value to the livability of a container home. Making sure that you position and orient windows in a way that maximizes the views you can capture requires some thought, but it's well worth it!

It's also interesting to think about the view from the inside, or what someone else (visitors, neighbors, or even your own family) would see if they looked inside. This is mostly about privacy and security concerns. You can have a problem if your neighbors can see into your bedroom or if your child's treehouse looks straight into your bathroom.

Another significant point to remember is the street view of your house. Changing the home's orientation in relation to the street can have a big impact on how it feels.

Some people prefer the house's long axis to be parallel to the street, whereas others prefer it to be perpendicular. If you have the room, you can place the house at an angle, enhancing the geometric design already provided by using containers.

Another option is to flip the design backward to change it up from what you originally planned.

You'll just have to see how much space you have for these options and how well they fit into your property and house design.

Setbacks and Restrictions

We spoke a lot about zoning and deed restrictions previously, and it's important to remember that these restrictions will impact where you build, even if it's on your land.

For example, the permissible height of your structure can be reduced as you get closer to a property line. Furthermore, you might be unable to build anything within a certain distance of a property line.

Before you commit to a construction site, make sure you consult with all relevant parties to ensure that what you're doing is legal. The longer you wait to find out, the costly it will be!

Access

The final part of the location requirements we'll discuss is site access. After all, a house is worthless if you can't get to it. Unless you're going completely off the grid, we'll presume that your primary mode of transportation would be via automobile, which means you will need a road. The easiest road to construct is one that is short, straight, and smooth, but this is not always possible due to land constraints.

Consider how you'll get to your potential building site from the main road on the edge of your property. How long will it be, and how much elevation change will there be? Are there any steep slopes that must be smoothed, low points that must be crossed, or natural obstacles that must be navigated around? What trees and other foliage would have to be cut down? Will the views improve or deteriorate as you travel up the lane, and will the changing seasons make the views better or worse?

Make sure you consider access not only for your vehicle, but also for building trucks, large trailers hailing containers, and heavy machinery such as cranes. Will the road be broad enough for them to use, with gentle enough turns? Will it be flat enough for them to walk over without high-centering? Will the mud and water render them impassable for heavy vehicles?

After considering all of these factors, you may decide to change the route of your access road slightly before you find one that best suits your needs. Note that if you can't come up with a single route that does it well, you can always build a second, temporary road for heavy machinery that will be demolished after the house is finished.

There are a variety of options for site access, but you don't want to be bushwhacking new trails the day a contractor arrives because your road is inadequate.

Site work

All of the physical work you'll have to do to get your construction site and surrounding area ready falls under the category of site work. It may make sense to do one before the other, depending on the type of dirt moving needed, the utilities you need to install, and the direction of approach, so you don't break something with heavy equipment.

Marking and Staking

The first step is to mark the corners of the area where your shipping container home will be built, as well as the locations of all planned and current utilities, roads, other buildings, and so on.

If you know you have water mains, gas pipelines, or other buried utilities that aren't connected with your project but simply transit through your property, you will need to hire a utility location company to help you with any of this.

Although special ground marking paint may be used in some situations, using wooden stakes is typically the better option. To get a better visual of larger areas, link them with string. You'll know exactly where you need to work on the following steps once you've marked out your building site.

Clearing and Grubbing

After that, clear the designated areas of foliage, debris, and obstacles. This involves clearing trees, bushes, rocks, junk, roots, and anything else in your way.

You can hire a contractor to do it, but if you want to save money, you should do it yourself. The more densely vegetated your area is, the more work it will be, and the more useful heavy machinery will be.

You must also consider what you will do with anything you accumulate. The vegetation could be broken up, with the small pieces being composted and the larger pieces being used as firewood. Alternatively, you might simply pile it up and burn, bury, or haul it away.

The rest of the garbage would most likely need to be collected and hauled to a dumpsite. You could pay someone to pick it up and dump it for you if you don't have access to a vehicle.

Grading, Cut, and Fill

Once you've cleared everything out of the way on your building site, you will start to see what you have to deal with. An uneven building site can be acceptable depending on the base you choose, as long as a crane can drop the containers onto it from a nearby location. However, if you want a slab or perimeter base, you'll need to grade and build a level building pad.

Now is also a perfect time to go over the drainage planning you did earlier. You may need to install swales and berms to regulate the flow of water, protect your container home, and divert water away from it.

You'll also need to make improvements to your access road. According to the discussion above, you should have chosen a route that is ideal for you and any contractors, but you might still need some surface prep work to smooth bumps and minimize steep grades. You may also need to build bridges, concrete low-water crossings, or culverts at any place where water flows.

Road Building

Road building is closely related to the last part of the previous segment. Although a road cut through the existing soil might be appropriate in certain circumstances, it is usually preferable to cover it with dirt, road base, asphalt, or even concrete to create a more stable, all-weather surface.

You may be able to wait, but keep in mind that heavy equipment trucks can seriously damage a dirt road, requiring you to return and regrade it later.

Erosion Control

The previous steps involved removing vegetation and moving dirt, all of which are ideal conditions for erosion to begin. Rain-induced erosion can cause unwanted sediment deposits on neighboring properties, sedimentation in ponds and streams, and loss of high-quality topsoil in the areas you cleared.

Planting an appropriate species of vegetation near the edge of where you cleared might be beneficial, but you'll need to leave the directly cleared areas bare in preparation for future construction activities.

As a result, temporary erosion control devices such as wattles, blankets, and silt fences must be used. These products won't stop erosion entirely, but they will keep them contained throughout the construction process.

Any of these options may be needed by law as part of a Storm Water Pollution Prevention Plan (SWPPP) or other similar planning document, depending on your area. More details should be available from the Environmental Quality office in your state or region.

Fencing and Security

Your project is progressing at this point, and you've most likely begun to spend money. You might also have tools and supplies that you'd like to leave on the work site when you're not working.

Our discussion of container locks and security is a good read on some of the ways to protect your container and the area around it.

Since you are unlikely to have your containers on-site at this time, not all of the recommendations in that section would apply to you.

For now, we suggest putting up a fence around the property. Now is an excellent time to build one if you intend to do so anyway. You can save money by clearing a fence line while you have the equipment on hand to clear the building site.

If a fence isn't feasible financially, a security camera or lighting can suffice. Your requirements are largely determined by the things you need to safeguard and the location of your house.

Planning for and Installing Utilities

Getting utilities to your construction site is critical not just for helping you to live in your container home, but also for making the building process go more smoothly. Without utilities, you will have to rely on water tanks, generators, and port-a-potties.

Although you'll usually have to contact each company separately, tools like in My Area will show you which companies (across several utility types) service your location. Check to see if all of the utilities have a monthly minimum fee. If that's the case, we suggest waiting to do the hookup until you are ready to begin construction. Doing it early would only result in you paying the minimum bill, regardless of whether you use it.

Some services may be deregulated, essentially monopolized by one company, or government-controlled, depending on where you live. If you have a choice as a customer between several companies that offer the same utility service, do some research to see which one is the better fit for your needs.

You can also see if they have any energy savings bonuses or rebates that you might qualify for with only a few changes to your design. Utilities can offer financial incentives to use better insulation and windows, as well as energy-efficient appliances, among other things. Be sure to ask!

Electricity

Electricity is the first and, arguably, most significant utility. Contact the nearest electrical cooperative or company to learn more about installing an electric meter and connecting to the power grid.

You should be able to get electrical service installed if there are power lines on the main road near your house. The cost will be determined by factors such as whether a new transformer is required, the duration (and difficulty) of the run, and whether it will be run underground or on poles. Typically, the company will have a set distance of wire and poles/trenching, beyond which you will be charged for every additional distance. They should be able to provide you with an estimate. Understand that they are also giving you a discount on the actual cost of installation with the expectation that they will benefit from your monthly service charge over time.

As a result, another issue you may face is the electrical company's desire to see some kind of improvement in your construction before committing to providing electrical service to your site. If they are unsure that you can finish the container home and become a loyal client, they will be hesitant to pay for the installation. Alternatively, they can encourage you to pay for a larger share of the cost yourself to minimize the risk. Each company is different, so find out what the requirements are in your area.

Understand that permits and approvals may be needed, especially with additional overhead poles that may affect neighbors. According to our previous point about minimum charges, you don't have to start the installation right away, but you can contact them as soon as possible to learn about the process and timeline.

You'll probably want to have temporary power installed first, which will provide you with a few electrical circuits, as part of the operation. It should be enough for the building, but it is insufficient for the entire house. The company will return after the house is completed to install your permanent service.

If commercial electric service isn't cost-effective, going off the grid with a generator, solar panels or wind turbine could be a better option than paying the electric company to extend service to you.

Gas

Gas is good for space heating, water heaters, and stoves, and includes natural gas or propane, a slightly less common alternative, propane. If you're in the city, you could have access to a natural gas line that you can tap into with a meter, similar to how electrical service is provided.

In more rural areas, you can normally rent or buy a big tank that stores gas which can last for months at a time.

It is best to find out gas prices in your region so you can make decisions about the appliances you want to use in your home. However, if gas is available, it is the most cost-effective and easiest to use.

Sewer and Septic

If your property has connections to nearby sewage lines, you'll need to find out how much it will cost and how long it will take to link. A septic system is likely your only choice in more rural areas.

A septic system would typically cost more to install than a sewer connection, but it will cost virtually nothing to use and maintain after the installation as compared to the monthly fee associated with your sewer connection.

A buried tank or tanks, as well as a buried line with leach pipes or sprinklers, are standard features of most septic systems. Work with your installer to come up with a suitable place for this equipment that will not obstruct potential development or livability.

Telecommunications

Although some people build shipping container houses in rural areas to get away from it all, most people prefer having at least some connectivity. The choices available vary greatly depending on your location.

You could have many options in the city, including cable, DSL, and fiber, which combine internet, television, and even phone service into a single bill. To get these services outside of the area, you may have to rely on satellite dishes, slower cable connections, or even point-to-point terrestrial radio frequency technology.

If you have a lot of options, make sure you call around and compare rates, and do some haggling. We'd also suggest talking to your neighbors to see what kind of approach they use and how they like it.

Early telecommunication access can be beneficial for tying in security camera surveillance, for example, and allowing fast Google searches or online shopping right from the building site!

Water

Water is last but not least. In the United States, the same water you use to bathe is also the water you drink, while in other nations, you'll need to buy potable bottled water separately. In any case, all but the most remote areas have access to a water source. If you can't get access for a reasonable price, you'll have to either dig a well or pay to get water trucked in and stored in a tank on site.

All of these solutions have higher initial costs, but if you plan on keeping your container home for a long time, they can be very affordable.

This in-depth discussion of required site planning activities should be a key step in the design and construction of a container home. Paying attention to this area would help you save money and transform a good home into a great home.

Chapter 4: SHIPPING CONTAINER HOME FOUNDATIONS

Along with the appropriate insulation, making sure you use the correct foundation for your shipping container home is crucial for a successful build.

Do I Need A Foundation For My Shipping Containers?

In short, you will always need a foundation for your shipping container home. This is because the ground moves a considerable amount. The ground can rise, sink or slide. This movement can be sporadic and is usually very slow. Even though it is often barely noticeable, this slight movement can affect how level your home is.

A foundation provides a solid, stable platform for your building. Without this solid platform, the ground's natural movement can cause the containers to split and separate. The ground underneath your building can also be comprised of different materials. For example, part of the ground could be hard rock, and the other part soft clay. This creates an unevenness that can allow your home to shift since the load isn't equally distributed. One result could be having doors that are incredibly difficult to open and close.

A solid, well-built, foundation will ensure the weight is appropriately distributed. It will also help prevent moisture and the corrosion that occurs as a result of this moisture.

Note that if the shipping container home will be relocated within a few months, it is sufficient to use railroad ties for this short time frame.

Types of Shipping Container Home Foundations

The four main foundation types which can be used with container homes are pier, pile, slab, and strip. There are other types of foundations but these are the most commonly used with container homes.

We will outline when you should use each one and discuss the strengths and weaknesses of each.

Making sure you use the proper foundation for your shipping container house, in addition to the proper insulation, is critical for a successful build.

Do I Need A Foundation For My Shipping Containers?

You will always need a foundation for your shipping container home. This is because the ground moves a lot. The ground has the ability to rise, sink, or slide. This movement can be intermittent and usually takes a long time. Even though it is mostly undetectable, this minor movement can affect the level of your house.

Your building's foundation provides a strong, secure basis. The natural movement of the ground will cause the containers to split and separate if there isn't a stable foundation in place.

The ground underneath your building can also be comprised of different materials. A part of the ground, for example, may be hard rock and the rest soft clay. Since the load isn't evenly distributed, this causes an unevenness that can cause your home to shift. As a result, it's possible that doors would be extremely difficult to open and close.

A solid, well-constructed foundation will ensure that the weight is distributed evenly. It will also aid in the prevention of moisture and the corrosion that results from it.

Note that if the shipping container home is only going to be moved for a few months, railroad ties will suffice.

Types of Shipping Container Home Foundations

The 4 main foundation types which can be used with container homes are pier, slab, strip, and pile. There are other types of foundations, but these are the most popular for container homes.

We'll go outline when you can use each one and discuss what their advantages and disadvantages are.

Pier Foundation

Pier foundations are the most common choice for shipping container homes for various reasons. They're cheap, DIY friendly, and quick to construct.

Courtesy of Larry Wade

A pier foundation is made up of concrete blocks, as seen in the image above. Each concrete block, or pier, is usually 50 cm X 50 cm X 50 cm in size and contains reinforcement steel on the inside to increase the concrete's tension strength. Concrete piers are usually laid at each corner of a shipping container house. Additionally, for larger 40-foot containers, two more piers can be mounted halfway down either side of the container.

Pier foundations save you a lot of time and money because you don't have to excavate a lot of earth at all. You only need to excavate ground for piers, which are usually 50 cm X 50 cm X 50 cm.

In contrast, a slab foundation requires the excavation of the entire area under the container.

Another good reason to use a pier foundation is that other foundations, such as pile foundations, require costly specialized equipment, which is difficult for DIY builders to obtain.

Concrete Piers

This is by far the most common shipping container foundation, and we recommend it.

Pile Foundations

Pile foundations are used when the soil type is too weak to support a concrete foundation. This is the most expensive form of foundation we've covered so far.

Pile foundations were used in the Graceville Container Home Case Study.

The piles (solid cylindrical steel tubes) are hammered into the soft soil until they meet more suitable load-bearing ground.

EXAMPLE OF PILE FOUNDATIONS

Once the piles have been secured in place they are usually capped with piles are usually covered with a block of concrete. So, after you've secured all of your piles, you'll have a grid structure of concrete caps that look like concrete piers above ground.

For a DIY builder, pile foundations are not recommended. contractor will be required to install pile foundations due to the specialized equipment required, such as the pile driver.

contractor will be required to install pile foundations due to the specialized equipment required, such as the pile driver.

Slab Foundation

When the ground is soft and an even weight distribution is needed, a slab foundation is a suitable choice. However, it takes longer and costs more to build than a pier foundation. Prepare to dig a lot if you're going to use a slab foundation.

A slab foundation, as seen in the picture above, is a concrete slab on which your containers are placed. The slab foundation is usually slightly wider than your home's footprint. If you're using two 40-foot shipping containers to build your home, your slab foundation should be 18 feet wide by 42 feet long. This will provide an overhanging foot of foundation around the circumference of your shipping containers.

The fact that slab foundations have a sturdy base means that there is no hollow space in the foundation. This prevents potential issues such as termite infestations.

Unfortunately, slab foundations are considerably more expensive than pier foundations due to the extra concrete used and a large amount of space that must be excavated. Slab foundations are often used in warmer climates where freezing isn't an issue. However, they increase the potential for heat loss when ground temperatures fall below the interior temperature, because the container will conduct heat into the ground, which transfers more heat than convection into the air.

With slab foundations, note that once the concrete has set, you won't be able to reach utility lines. If you leak your water pipe, you'll need to break the concrete to get to it. You'll still have access to your utility lines with a pier foundation.

Strip Foundation

A strip foundation (also called trench foundation) is a combination of the pier and slab foundations mentioned previously.

The strip foundation, as seen below, is nothing more than a concrete strip laid to support the containers. Usually, the concrete strip is 1-2 feet wide and 4 feet deep.

The strip may be laid along the perimeter of the containers or at the top and bottom instead.

It's a good choice if you want a cheaper alternative to a slab foundation but has a little less firm ground to lay the foundation on.

A rubble strip foundation with loose stone under the concrete strip can be used in areas where the ground remains damp for long periods due to heavy rain. The water will pass through this stone and drain away.

Strip foundations, like all of the other foundation forms listed, have weaknesses. Strip foundations, for instance, have poor earthquake resistance. Strip foundations are also ideally suited for small and medium-sized buildings due to their shallow shape.

How to Attach Shipping Containers to Foundations

A steel plate is the most common method of attaching containers to the foundation pad. The cast-in-place option involves pushing a steel plate into wet concrete with welded anchors underneath. After the concrete has set, you could epoxy the anchors into it. Mechanical anchors are also an option, but they are usually less strong and are not recommended.

In either case, you'll need a flat, level concrete plate to fit the four corner fittings on each container. The shipping containers are mounted on the steel plates after the concrete has cured, and everything can be welded together.

Some people choose to simply put the containers on the foundations, relying on their massive weight to keep them in place. This is generally good in most situations, but keep in mind that floods and tornadoes can easily lift a loose container!

The Strength of Concrete to Use for Your Foundation

This section is particularly important if you want to build on a concrete pier or a slab foundation.

When people decide to use a concrete foundation, the next question they usually have is what concrete strength to use. The geo-technical engineer's report will determine the strength of concrete you'll need for your foundation.

The concrete strength will be referred to as a C value. 1 part cement, 2 parts sand, and 5 parts gravel are used to make C15 concrete, a general all-purpose concrete. The heavier the concrete is, the more cement it contains. C30, for instance, is a very strong concrete consisting of one part cement, two parts sand, and three parts gravel.

If you're just mixing a small quantity of concrete, you can do it by hand or with a cement mixer. If you need more than 1 cubic meter, consider getting concrete shipped directly to your site, ready to use.

If you're mixing the concrete yourself, make sure you thoroughly mix all of the elements; otherwise, the strength of the concrete would be significantly reduced.

Simply calculate the cubic meters of your foundation to decide how much concrete you'll need. Multiply the width, height, and depth together.

Multiply 10 x 22 x 2 to find the amount of concrete needed for a 10-foot wide, 22-foot long, 2-foot deep slab foundation. A total of 440 cubic feet of concrete will be needed.

The cement will begin to cure after it has been mixed with water. Make sure the concrete cures properly since this increases its strength and durability. The temperature of the concrete must be maintained within a certain range to cure properly (refer to the manufacturer's packaging).

The concrete cures in 5-7 days on average. It must be kept moist throughout this period.

Pouring Concrete in Hot Weather

If you are laying concrete in hot weather, it's important to properly prepare the site before pouring the concrete. Place temporary sun shades over the concrete to block any direct sunlight. You should also spray the ground with cold water before laying the concrete. Make sure you use cold water when mixing the concrete.

It's also a good idea to pour the concrete later in the evening or first thing in the morning to avoid peak temperatures.

Pouring Concrete in Cold Weather

When pouring concrete in cold weather, special precautions must be taken just like pouring concrete in hot weather. Cold weather is classed as the average temperature falls below freezing for more than three consecutive days. Make sure all snow or ice has been removed from the foundation and forms before pouring the concrete. Remove any water that has accumulated. Once you've laid your concrete, cover it with insulating blankets as soon as possible. Use the blankets for three to seven days while the concrete is curing. Remove the blankets gradually after the concrete has cured to avoid the concrete cracking due to rapid temperature changes.

You now understand why you need a foundation in the first place and how to choose the best one for your project. You should be able to mix the cement for this type of foundation. Make sure you pay close attention to the instructions for laying in extremely hot and cold temperatures, as this can make or break your container's foundation.

Chapter 5:
EXTERIOR FINISH

Despite their apparent toughness, cargo shipping containers seem to blend in seamlessly with new, twenty-first-century architecture. In fact, metal combined with glass now makes up a significant portion of urban architecture. With this in mind, the idea of residential houses with metal structures rather than conventional wooden-frame ones does not seem so strange.

The speed at which containers made their way into residential construction. As it turned out, these otherwise uninspiring, shadowy corrugated steel blocks opened up new dimensions to the art of structural design, allowing us to enter the familiar realm of fantasies from Legoland, where our imagination is the only limit. By rotating, tilting, shifting individual CorTen-steel blocks, combining glass with metal, and adding vivid colors, suddenly, these boringly looking, clearly lifeless industrial structures began new episodes of vibrant this time. The trend got so powerful that it gained its name – Cargotecture.

Escape Den: The rustic romanticism that containers evoke is taken delightfully by architects to recreate a place that is impeccably out of the world, almost surreal. Source: River and Rain (Bangladesh), photos by Hasan Chandan & Maruf Raihan

Joshua Tree Home rising from the ground in Californian desert is an example of modern cargotecture perfectly blending with the surrounding nature. Source: Whitaker Studio (UK)

The Escape Den, which is slowly drowning in the late-evening darkness, and the Space Odyssey-like Joshua Tree with its arms bursting into the open sky, prove that impossible is a thing of the past. In the hands of skilled architects, dull blocks of painted steel were transformed into works of art that blended seamlessly into the surrounding landscape. The Beast as it turned out has quite an unexpected face – the Beauty.

The bottom line is that rugged corrugated steel boxes give rise to stylishness, elegance, and a dash of extravagance. The common feature of these designs is the luck of traditional siding, which, in addition to protecting from the elements, is also used to beautify the structure's appearance.

Most containers do not require any additional weather protection cladding. Corten steel is self-sealing (a thin film of oxidation protects the underlying metal from corrosion), and the paint coating adds extra protection.

However, there are times when container-based structures require exterior cladding.

a. Visual harmony with the environment (be it urbane ambiance, nature, or local neighborhood).

Local governments can impose such requirements, or nature-conscious property owners can impose them on themselves to reduce the visual impact of their intrusion into nature.

b. Exterior insulation

The advantages of exterior insulation can sometimes outweigh its technical complexity and extra cost. First, it is the gained interior space (especially noticeable in cold climate zones where the insulation must be thick to minimize the cost of heating). Second, by moving the thermal insulation to the outside of the walls, we eliminate the effect of vapor condensation, which is typically difficult to avoid when the insulation is built inside the structure.

c. Personal Touch

This includes situations where you want to add personal touches to your container-based home regardless of backdrop and local ambiance. The shrewd use of various materials, grains, colors, and panel orientations can highlight the structure's specific architecture, distinguishing it from the "pack." It's a sort of an individual, loudly pronounced public statement that lasts!

THIS 1,500 SQ. FT RESIDENCE IS ANCHORED ON A ROCK OUTCROP TO TAKE FULL ADVANTAGE OF PANORAMIC VIEWS. THE EXTERIOR CLADDING IS A COMBINATION OF DIFFERENT MATERIALS, THEIR GEOMETRICAL ORIENTATIONS, AND COLORS. SOURCE: TOMECEK STUDIO ARCHITECTURE (PHOTOS BY BRADEN GUNEM).

Popular Cladding materials for containers:

Only a few of the commonly used cladding materials in the residential housing industry find applications for containers. Understandably, low-cost vinyl siding isn't the most exciting choice for containers. On the other hand, some more expensive sidings, such as stone, brick, or stucco, which are often used in higher-end residential constructions, are not only inefficient and labor-intensive but also "not in tune" with cargotecture's distinct design.

Since container metal walls are impermeable, it's critical to make the exterior layer of cladding breathable. Any water vapor or moisture that may inadvertently penetrate the space between the external cladding and the container's wall would be able to escape in good weather.

Because CorTen steel is not 100 percent corrosion proof, most insulations are permeable and susceptible to mold and mildew, and the supporting wooden frame may eventually rot, the accumulated moisture will weaken the structure.

In practice, the choice of material(s) for container house exterior cladding is influenced not only by aesthetics (which includes texture, colors, finish, geometrical profiles, and so on), but also by cost (labor and materials), R-factor (if part of the overall insulation strategy), durability, and maintenance requirements.

Timber

Timber has been used as the main building material in residential housing for a long time, mostly in the form of logs. It's no surprise that wood is regaining popularity as an exterior cladding material, thanks to the recent trend of "getting closer to nature" (of which container-based houses are a big part). Painted or stained offers classy elegance much sought in urban ambiance. Timber cladding can softly blend with nature in the countryside due to its rustic appearance, mitigating the effects of "human interference." In both cases, wood adds a sort of visually enhanced warmness into undistinguishable, colorless structures. Timber is, of course, a sustainable and environmentally friendly material! Canadian Western Red Cedar and Redwood (both), as well as Larch (especially Canadian and Siberian), chestnut, and oak, are the most common types of wood used for exterior cladding (last three belonging to the class of hardwood). All of these species share characteristics that make them suitable for outdoor use in their natural state. They have a high resistance to decay and rot due to the presence of tannins. Additionally, due to their much higher density than larch, chestnut, softwood, and oak are more resistant to moisture, termites, and decaying organisms, making them more resilient in outdoor applications.

They're all available in a range of warm light colors, from golden to reddish, making them ideal for exterior cladding. Unfortunately, as they age, their original colors fade into an unappealing greyish shade. That is why usually they are painted or stained to preserve their original warmness. Unfortunately, those coatings deteriorate over time, so here's the brutal truth of timber: it needs to be re-coated every three to five years (depending on the type of coating). To add insult to injury, another disadvantage is that the timber is extremely flammable! Timber, unfortunately, loses its "innocence" when treated with flame retardants (health hazard).

Timber designed for external cladding comes in different styles and profiles – shingles, lapboards, boards, board, and batten, half-logs, designed for overlapping or joining using tongue and groove, etc.). Note that timber is relatively simple to mount, and the variety of forms available allows for the production of additional visual effects (for example horizontally installed boards will optically elongate the structure while vertical ones will make it look taller). Although the natural color of wood is typically preferred, wood is one of the few cladding materials that allows for color customization to match the owner's personal preferences.

It's worth noting that timber has excellent thermal and sound insulation properties, which are both essential in container homes.

The Helm – two-story container home combines cedar sidings with sections of original corrugated steel. Source: Cargo Home (TX, USA)

20ft Container-based cabin with rustic-style log cladding. Source: Custom Container Living (Missouri, USA)

Cedar is, without a doubt, the most common choice for timber cladding, not only because of its natural beauty and wide range of colors (from white to yellow, red to brown); however, also because of its distinct, pleasant aroma (aroma). The reality is that, despite significant advances in composite and engineered-wood material quality, Mother Nature can only be imitated, not replaced.

Cedar cladding is a practical solution because it is naturally resistant to rot and insects, does not warp in the presence of moisture and lasts for a long time in outdoor applications without the use of chemicals.... Yes, it is costly, but if properly sealed and preserved, it will serve you for many years, greeting you with gracious natural beauty every day!

To be clear, all wood is biodegradable, so in wet climate zones, if cedar cladding is not properly maintained (cleaning and sealing with stain or paint), mold may inevitably grow, causing the cladding to rot. It's a natural process, and we should agree that all "natural" creations have gone through millions of years of proving "tests" before receiving Mother Nature's final blessing, so the rot is also a time-proven process! This stands in contrast with the men-made "designs" that emerge from the factory doors, with men-written certificates that often prove to be worthless.

Note that cedar is a fast-growing tree (only bamboo grows faster), so it's a truly sustainable resource. The entire manufacturing process, including harvesting, transportation, and processing (cutting the boards), uses a fraction of the energy needed for the production of composite cladding materials.

The entire manufacturing process, including harvesting, transportation, and processing (cutting the boards), uses a fraction of the energy needed for the production of composite cladding materials. Timber Protection

Raw wood will decay over time, regardless of its natural resistance to weather elements and insects, When exposed to sunlight (especially UV) and moisture. The first effects would be purely visual, with natural colors gradually turning grayish, but this is also a sign of the beginning of the deterioration process. Coating – either with stain or paint – is the most common method of protection.

Stain seems to be a better solution since it penetrates deeper layers of wood. The stain becomes an integral part of the wood's close-to-surface layers as a result of this penetration, and it will not peel off like paints. The latter creates a thin film on the surface of wood, so it is more prone to peeling and cracking.

There are several versions of stain:

1. Surface Stains (water-based) – breathable, great for vertical cladding, offer excellent UV protection, have excellent adhesion to fibers of wood.

2. Hybrid Stains (based on water in emulsions of drying oils) – partly breathable, excellent UV protection, can penetrate shallow layers of wood, but leave a thin film on the wood's surface that can peel and crack.

3. Deep-Penetrating Stains (based on non-drying oils) – water-impermeable (not breathing) penetrate deep layers of wood, prone to crack and peel, have poor UV tolerance (so their colors will quickly fade).

Notes:

• Breathable coating allows the water to escape from the timber. Rainwater will inevitably penetrate behind the cladding because "all sealed joints are leaking" (Murphy laws). Furthermore, each piece of raw wood (if not aged and dried) will have some water trapped inside, which will cause rotting.

•, Unlike paints, stains can only be applied to raw, untreated, and unpainted wood.

As an example, we'd like to point out an "unorthodox" method of protecting the timber from the elements. It's based on the "Shou-Sugi-Ban" Japanese wood waterproofing technique, which is both old and tested. It involves charring the surface of the wood with open flames from a blowtorch for a short period. Once a black layer of charcoal has formed, it should be washed with a wire brush to remove any loose particles, dusted with compressed air, and finally sealed. If left unprotected, the charred wood is said to last for 80 to 100 years (longer if coated with oil for protection). There is science behind the Shou-Sugi-Ban method: high temperatures shrink wood cells, resulting in a protective layer with a greatly reduced ability to absorb moisture and higher resistance to decay.

Phases of Shou-Sugi-Ban method: correspondingly deeply charred pine wood (left), cleaned with a wire brush (center), and sanded (right). Source: Eastern White Pine

It's incredible, but to be clear, not all woods are suitable for this process. Originally, it was used on cedarwood in Japan because it has specific natural chemical components that make this method more effective. However, it appears that the Shou-Sugi-Ban methods can work well on maple, cypress, oak, and even pine. Here's the evidence:

FIRST STEP OF WATERPROOFING: CHARRING THE SURFACE OF THE CEDARWOOD

The Final effect – custom exterior yellow cedar siding was finished with a Japanese wood-burning technique shou-sugi-ban. (Location: Whitehorse, YT, Canada). Source: Northern Front Studio (Canada)

Bamboo

Bamboo is the fastest-growing tree on the planet, making it a completely sustainable resource. It's worth noting that giant bamboo stems are ready for harvesting after about four to six years of growth, while hardwood takes tens of years. Furthermore, bamboo plants can regrow new stems after being removed, preventing deforestation. Bamboo, in its natural form of hollow stems, may be used for decorative cladding. When exposed to moisture, they do not swell or warp, and they are very robust, but they can lose their natural colors and mildew. That's why bamboo stems for outdoor use are normally processed and coated to prevent fading.

Decorative cladding of the shipping container house made from bamboo screens (stems were treated using the "Burn-and-Wax" process based on an old Japanese "Shou Sugi Ban" technique used for waterproofing and preserving the wood). Source: Bamboo Suppliers of Ireland (Project commissioned for Ceardean Architects)

Hollow bamboo stems are usually split along their lengths and steamed to retain their natural (light yellow) color or thermally treated to obtain a dark brown color after the outer skin is removed. Individual bamboo strips are then compressed to build sturdy, high-density outdoor boards. In sharp contrast to natural woods, one of the leading companies (MOSO-Bamboo) claims that their bamboo boards designed for exterior cladding not only have the highest hardness, durability, and stability over time but also meet relevant fire-safety criteria without any chemical treatments! The bottom line is that this environmentally friendly, fast-growing wood stays Ecological forever.

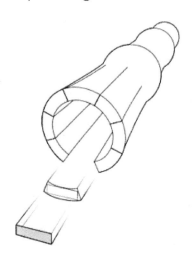

plain pressed (PP)
Strips are placed horizontally and glued together to create a wide line pattern with the characteristic bamboo nodes clearly visible.

side pressed (SP)
Strips are placed vertically and glued together to create a narrow line pattern with the bamboo nodes visible in a subtle way.

high density* (HD)
Strips are compressed and glued under high pressure,

THE FIRST STEP IN THE PROCESSING IS TO STRIP THE HOLLOW BAMBOO STEM ALONG ITS LENGTH. AFTER BEING TREATED AND DRIED, THE STRIPS CAN BE CONNECTED IN SEVERAL WAYS TO MAKE THE FINAL PRODUCT. ENGINEERED PANELS MADE FROM "BAKED" BAMBOO STRIPS MAINTAIN THEIR ORIGINAL COLOR FOR MUCH LONGER THAN TRADITIONAL TIMBER. THEY ARE DURABLE AND WEATHER RESISTANT UNTIL SEALED WITH OILS (WITH ANTI-MOLD AND ROT PROTECTION), MAKING THEM AN EXCELLENT OPTION FOR OUTDOOR APPLICATIONS. ENGINEERED BAMBOO PANELS ARE AN EXCELLENT ECOLOGICAL ALTERNATIVE TO THE COMMONLY USED

CONVENTIONAL TIMBER, DESPITE THEIR LACK OF POPULARITY. THE SAD REALITY IS THAT SINCE LONG THE HARVEST OF TROPICAL TREES BECAME UNSUSTAINABLE. UNFORTUNATELY, SINCE THE TROPICS ARE TOO FAR FROM THE CENTERS OF THE WESTERN WORLD, IT'S EASIER TO PRETEND THAT DEFORESTATION DOESN'T EXIST (SOME WILL SAY IT HAPPENS SOMEWHERE ELSE, SO WHO CARES, FORGETTING THAT WE HAVE ONLY ONE EARTH).

Examples of bamboo cladding (left) and decking (right).
Source: BothBest Bamboo Flooring Co. Ltd (China)

Most manufacturers of bamboo claddings provide some kind of "Clip & Lock" systems that makes the installation easy.

Cladding from compressed bamboo strips (here also used for patio floor). Source: MOSO-Bamboo

Engineered Wood

Engineered wood combines natural wood's highly prized aesthetics (color, texture, warmth, etc.) with the toughness and weather resistance of man-made composite materials. Engineered wood, also known as WPC (Wood-Plastic-Composite), is made up of around 50% wood flour (powdered wood fibers), 35-to-40% HDPE plastic (High-Density Polyethylene), and 10–15 percent other additives. HDPE is regarded as a component that poses no health risks (does not contain BPA and is approved for use by the food industry). Much less is known about additives (bonding and color agents, among other things), but because we're talking about outdoor applications, off-gassing might not be an issue. The bottom line is that engineered wood now provides the best of two worlds. WPC boards are weather-resistant (no mildew, mold, or rot), UV-resistant, and most likely non-toxic, but the latter attribute is highly dependent on the manufacturer's "recipe," so check applicable certifications before making a purchase. WPC boards, unlike conventional wood, are fireproof (well, additives once again, because HDPE and powdered wood fibers are flammable). Engineered wood is available in a wide range of designs, textures, shapes, and colors (most manufacturers will imitate traditional timber like red pine, larch, cedar, redwood, but will also offer a selection of colors including custom choices). It doesn't need to be maintained (there's no need to paint or stain it, so no peeling or cracks...). Engineered wood, on the other hand, CANNOT be painted or stained, so once you've chosen it and built it, you won't be able to alter its appearance or feel (in other words, the advantages of "maintenance-free" comes with strings attached). The good news is that engineered wood panels are, for the most part, recyclable (if one day you will decide to get rid of them).

EXAMPLES OF ENGINEERED WOOD PANELS DESIGNED FOR EXTERIOR WALLS CLADDING. SOURCE: COOWIN GROUP

Engineered wood exterior cladding. Source: COOWIN Group

Fiber-Cement boards

Fiber-cement boards are made from a combination of concrete (Portland cement and sand) and cellulose fibers, as well as some "additives" (fillers, aluminum stearate, polyvinyl alcohol (PVA), pigments, mica, and so on...). Concrete makes up roughly 50-60% of total volume, fibers used to strengthen the concrete makeup 10%, and fillers – usually cenospheres (lightweight, hollow spheres of alumina or silica filled with air) – make up 30%. They're used to make fiber-cement boards lighter (and denser). The components are pressed together to create a rigid, homogeneous material. Fiber-cement boards, in general, are environmentally friendly since they are constructed from renewable materials.

Fiber-cement panels are UV-resistant, weather-resistant, rot- and insect-resistant, fire-resistant, and extremely solid (although their impact resistance may not be their strongest point). They come in a variety of shapes, colors, and textures, from smooth to visibly textured. As a result, fiber-cement boards can convincingly imitate other cladding materials such as timber (the most common design), but also bricks, stones, and tiles at a much lower initial cost. It's worth noting that fiber-cement boards aren't "cheap imitations," as we normally refer to low-quality replacement parts; in fact, their appearance may be very similar to that of real timber in many instances.

While fiber-cement boards are normally pre-colored, they can be repainted after installation, making them more appealing.

House with painted fiber-cement cladding. Source: Architizer (Lewin Residence (Atlanta, GA, USA)

Notes:

The natural gray color of concrete is preserved with uncoated fiber-cement boards. They are breathable in their natural raw state, meaning they can be penetrated by vapor and moisture. If the cladding is only used to improve the aesthetics of the container structure, it will not cause any problems. But, due to the exposure to the elements, efflorescence can occur over time (migration of salts to the surface of porous materials and their permanent deposition when moisture evaporates). If the fiber-cement cladding is being used to secure exterior insulation, both sides should be sealed (transparent paint or stain to preserve the look). Another option is to use a Tyvek-type moisture barrier as a protective envelope behind the cladding.

The vast majority of fiber-cement boards are sealed from the factory (usually by water-based acrylic paints). These coatings provide weather resistance (UV, mold, moisture, etc.) as well as durability and efflorescence resistance. Unlike timber and engineered wood, standard fiber-cement cladding has a low R-factor and therefore does not contribute to the overall insulation benefit of the container. Acoustic insulation is often used in conjunction with thermal insulation. You'll need to install an acoustic barrier behind the fiber-cement cladding if it's needed. Given that metal structures have a propensity to echo in the presence of noise, it may be a requirement in an industrial or city setting where a wide range of loud noise is generated. This should not be an issue in rural areas.

Fiber-cement boards, like many other claddings, are built with tongue and groove systems or by overlapping (horizontal lap sidings).

Fiber-cement boards – horizontal overlapping siding. Source: North Knox Siding and Windows (USA)

Cladding with fiber cement panels. Source: Architizer (Beach House designed by Levenbetts)

Composite materials

Composite materials are made up of at least two (and sometimes many more) separate substances (materials) that work together to make a composite that is better and stronger products than each component alone. Mother Nature has produced countless examples of organic composite materials in her relentless "battle for survival." Humans have advanced this art and science significantly in the last 100 years, creating a plethora of synthetic composite materials. They gradually became a part of our lives to the point that we now consider them to be still present in our everyday lives. This new class of man-made composites has "engineered" properties that enable them to be used almost anywhere, from home to space applications.

Composite materials are suitable for outdoor applications due to characteristics such as lightweight, strength, weather resistance (UV, moisture, high and low temperatures...), corrosion, mold, mildew resistance, staining & discoloration resistance, resilience, durability, low wear & tear impact, low maintenance.... (and the list goes on and on). It's no surprise that composite materials are used for exterior cladding.

The list of their weaknesses isn't long (although they may heavily weigh on our decisions). There are the following:

Typically, there is a high initial cost (sometimes it can be justified by low or no maintenance costs, elegance, and durability)

Many composite materials are non-biodegradable and therefore not environmentally friendly.

However, for completeness, we must note that the industry offers a plethora of composite materials that are ideal for exterior claddings not only because of the characteristics listed above, but also because of their beauty, style, and ability to closely match the appearance of natural cladding materials.

Perfect imitation of stone. Source: Archiproducts

Corian cladding (to most of us associated with kitchen countertops, here underlines the architectural beauty of this modern building). Source Archiproducts

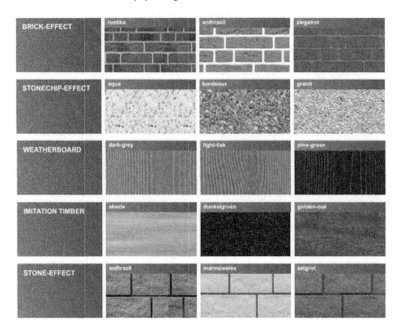

Selection of composite claddings (fragment). Source: Container Clad (UK)

Note: Engineered wood and fiber-cement siding are often referred to as composite materials. Despite the fact that they are "composite materials" (i.e., mixtures of different components), we chose to present them separately due to the differences in their makeup, popularity, appearance, and suitability for container cladding.

Composite Panels

Sandwiches of thick layers of insulation between laminated metal sheets are used to make composite panels (typically aluminum or steel). As a result, they're often referred to as Sandwich Panels. Although they may be used as a combined integral layer of cladding AND insulation for exterior siding, they are most commonly used to construct load-bearing walls. Composite panels are almost exclusively used for the construction of Customized Container Houses. They frequently use corrugated metal on the exterior side of the sandwich to mimic cargo shipping containers. When it comes to core insulation, manufacturers typically provide a wide range of materials such as Polyurethane or Polystyrene Foams, Mineral Wool, Fiberglass, and so on, with thicknesses varying depending on the R-factor needed.

Metal sheets are factory-coated with polyester, polyvinylidene fluoride (PVDF), silicone polyester, polyvinyl chloride (PVC), acrylic paints, etc. Given their coated-metal finish, composite panels are weather-resistant (moisture, rain, vapor, UV...), mildew, mold, and rot-resistant, insect resistant, durable, require little maintenance (though dusty environments can necessitate washing), and their initial colors do not fade over time.

On the negative side, it's essentially metal siding, and while there are attempts to mimic the wood, it'll be obvious even from afar that this isn't the case! They may also be very expensive.

Composite Panels (here rock-wool insulation sandwiched in aluminum). Source: Xiamen Zhongjingtai Building Materials

Co., Ltd.

EXAMPLE OF THE COMPOSITE (SANDWICH) PANEL WITH POLYURETHANE RESIN (PUR) INSULATION. SOURCE: ARCHIPRODUCTS (USA)

Metal

Although it can seem strange to add extra metal cladding to the metal container walls, such solutions may often be beneficial. The main one is normally – adding an exterior layer of thermal insulation while maintaining the metal envelope's weather-related benefits. After all, metal cladding is UV, insects, weather, fire (and the list goes on...) resistant, as well as strong and durable. Metal does not require much maintenance other than regular washing, testing for corrosion (if steel), and re-painting if necessary.

Metal claddings are made from aluminum, zinc, stainless

steel, copper, brass, Corten steel, or standard steel, while containers are often made of CorTen steel (or an equivalent) (the latter must be powder-coated or galvanized to prevent corrosion). Copper or copper alloys are valued for their weathered greenish patina, but they are costly. Corten steel may also be used for exterior cladding. Corten steel develops a rusty-reddish-brownish patina under "normal circumstances" (moderate, dry climate zone) that form a thin layer of firm coating that prevents deeper corrosion. Corrosion is almost unstoppable in salty and wet environments like shore locations (particularly in warm climate zones).

Corten-like "BlueScope Weathering Steel" cladding. Source: Metal Cladding Systems (Australia)

Metal cladding, as previously said, cannot be mistaken for anything else. It will provide a smooth, aesthetic surface that is highly predictable in any color you choose. Metal cladding can reflect a portion of sunlight, reducing the overheating effect, as compared to timber (or any porous cladding material). It's worth noting that firsthand experience can be deceiving because metals transmit heat almost immediately, while timber absorbs far more heat energy and requires more time.

Manufacturers sell a wide range of profiles for horizontal, vertical, and diagonal claddings, as well as tailored shapes (for bends, curves, and so on) and a variety of seam/inter-locking systems, all in a large palette of colors.

METAL CLADDING. SOURCE: LIVINBIGINATINYHOUSE (3X 20FT SHIPPING CONTAINERS...)

Cladding Installation

Installing cladding (along with a layer of insulation) on the outside of container walls is more difficult than it is for conventional wooden-frame houses. The lack of a pressboard (as a matter of fact any wooden components) supporting installation with staples or nails is what makes a major difference (and complicates the process).

Metal screws are not just inconvenient and time-consuming to use. The airtightness (or rather, impermeability) of the entire system would be jeopardized by holes in the walls. One might argue that the installation of doors, vents, windows, and other airtight equipment has already removed the airtightness, but airtightness (hermeticity) is not the preferred state of the habitable space. The truth is that moisture, air, and water infiltration along the window and door frames can be seen and eliminated. The mounting holes would be uniformly distributed around the walls, making them virtually invisible and inaccessible for inspection. And that is what makes the painful difference.

The bottom line is that there is no easy solution to this problem so far. In the vast majority of instances, you'll need to build a supporting frame (usually from the treated wood). Some people would only use glue to attach the wooden frame (2 by "whatever is appropriate") to the corrugated walls, maintaining the container's integrity in this way. DIY guys may add a few metal screws for added safety, and others that use more complicated frame designs that take advantage of already existing holes designed for lifting cargo shipping containers during transport. It all depends on your creativity, expertise, and time constraints.

a. Cladding only

Adding additional cladding for aesthetic purposes just makes the job easier. It's because there's no risk of air penetration between the structural walls and the cladding. Leaving a small gap between the container's (structural) walls and the exterior cladding will allow air to circulate through convection. It's worth noting that air sucked from the ground level would most likely be cooler than air sucked from the upper level of walls. This natural passive ventilation can aid in reducing the effects of overheating caused by direct sun exposure.

For practical reasons, you'll need a supporting (most likely wooden) frame for practical purposes, but it can be built so that it's just loosely attached to the container's framework. the frame can be attached with adhesives if necessary, but bolting it to the container structure is not justified. After all, the aim is to mimic the appearance of traditional cladding materials, colors, and textures without putting additional strain on the container's structure or jeopardizing its integrity.

Some cladding system manufacturers have already resolved these issues by providing self-supporting cladding frames (Container Clad, Lion Containers, and so on...).

b. Cladding over exterior insulation

Adding external insulation complicates matters. You don't want any air to get behind the cladding, particularly between the insulation layer and the container walls. In the first case, you'll risk the deterioration of insulation when exposed to moisture.   In the second case, exterior air infiltration would create "heat bridges," negating the advantages of the external thermal insulation.

Closed-cell spray foam insulations are particularly useful for outdoor applications. They stick securely to metal walls, are virtually impermeable, and have a high R-factor, despite their high cost. They will also grow mold/mildew if exposed to moisture, so it may be necessary to install breathable cladding to allow moisture and water vapor to escape.

Off-gassing (one of the popular reasons against the use of spray-foams) is largely insignificant in this case because it happens outdoors!

Adhesives with bolting

Adhesives may not pass the test of time, the frame will need to be bolted to the structural walls at least in a few places for safety.

Welded metal tabs

Although it is unlikely to be a DIY job, you can preserve the integrity of container walls (no holes). After the taps are welded along with the container's upper, middle, and lower perimeters, you can bolt horizontal 2 by 4s in place and then nail vertical cladding boards.

Note that in both cases, an overhanging roof is needed to prevent rainwater infiltration behind the cladding (particularly important if you also installed the insulation).

One of the possible methods of installation of the cladding (first batons are attached horizontally to the structural walls, then the Siberian Larch cladding is installed vertically using traditional methods (screws). Source: ContainersDirect

Chapter 6: HOW TO JOIN CONTAINERS

Why People Connect Shipping Containers: The Benefits

To Create Larger Interior Spaces or Clear-Spans

The most significant advantage of combining two shipping containers is the increased customizability and space. This allows you to make the most of your shipping container's interior space, which is particularly appealing when creating a shipping container home, office, retail store, or simply a larger storage unit. It is, however, more of a storage garage of this size.

The following are some of the advantages of combining containers for extra space:

• Customize the space dimensions and partitions to your preference.

• Segmentation gives the interior of a typical building structure a traditional feel.

• Customers and staff can feel less cramped with wider shipping container structures.

Take Advantage of Their "Modular" or "Volumetric Shape"
Shipping containers are identical to modular or prefabricated volumetric building components in terms of construction. Because of their volumetric form, they can be conveniently stacked and placed side by side on the construction site. The convenient stacked and connecting can be used to build any width or height that the structure is permitted to handle.

You may also hire a company to do all of the requisite construction off-site and then ship the finished containers to your campus. This reduces finishing and on-site construction time, allowing for more predictable schedules and costs.

Finance a Large Building – One Shipping Container at a Time
Due to the relative ease with which shipping containers can be joined together and stacked, you can budget out a housing or commercial building project based on your current funding and budget criteria. Begin by attaching a few shipping containers for your new house, and as your savings or income grows, you can add more shipping containers to your project at any time.

How to Join Two Shipping Containers Together

There are several ways that Individuals across different industries and requirements choose to connect shipping containers. We're often asked about welding them together and stacking container limits. We'll go over how shipping containers are often connected below, and then we'll address some of the frequently asked questions.

Step 1: Develop layout plans with the help of a licensed contractor for spec advice.

Have a comprehensive plan or design in place before you get too wrapped up in building a clear-span space for your shipping containers – this involves possible add-ons. This method of preparation ensures that everyone involved in the process is aware of the project's requirements and specifications.

It also helps you to consult with or hire contractors who will help you preserve the integrity of your shipping containers when you begin to adjust them for assembly.

Step 2) Before the joining process, modifications to shipping container walls should be made.

If you are dealing with multiple standard shipping containers, you will need to modify the walls first. This is especially true if you choose to remove any or all of the interior walls to build doorways or a completely open room. Beams and bracing columns can be installed as necessary and in consideration with potential add-ons.

You should also make sure to neatly frame in any openings you've made in your shipping container walls to help create a uniform and tight seal between containers.

You may also want to think about the benefits of buying an open side container since their wide doorways are already framed. Simply remove the doors for open space.

Step 3) Site Preparation for the Containers

Make sure all units' foundations are compacted and perfectly level. This will help you maintain a clean, standardized structure and, once again, build the best seal.

Assemble the first unit and place it on the foundation. Before you begin to position the second unit, make sure the first unit is completely straight and in place.

Place the second unit in place and repeat the measurements. It's important that everything lines up perfectly because changing the location of the shipping containers after they've been connected would be incredibly difficult.

Step 4) Joining the Shipping Containers Together

Plates and caulking are one of the most popular ways to bind shipping containers to ensure that the seam between them is well-connected.

Tools Required:

- Threshold plates
- Drill
- Screws
- Caulk
- Flashing

Now that your shipping containers are positioned together, you can start the connection process by placing threshold plates along the seam. Make sure you use screws to keep them in place.

Threshold plates and flashing (roof) can be used to cover the seams on the walls and ceiling on the exterior of the container.

Step 5) Use caulk, roofing cement, or welding to make a good seal.

Finally, most people would use caulk to help seal the container against the elements and improve performance. A ridge cap, along with additional roofing cement and roofing materials, will help protect the roof of your new two-container home.

Can you weld two shipping containers together?

Yes, indeed. If you have welding experience, this is a more permanent way of joining 2 shipping containers together.

Can You Stack Containers Vertically?

Yes, but make sure the weight is spread mainly through the corner posts so that the foundation takes the brunt of the load. We strongly advise using structural engineers and architects when constructing a multi-story shipping container building to avoid catastrophic collapses.

Tips for Joining Shipping Containers Together

If you're joining two or more shipping containers to make a container home or business, you'll probably need to install a few new support columns on the inside to ensure structural integrity. As a result, you'll need to use more space in your interior design plans.

Why do you need additional support? When perfectly welded together, the roofs of the two shipping containers would technically be joined. This distributes more weight than the original configuration of any shipping container predicted. When snow or rain piles on top of the roof, adding a few interior support columns will ensure that it does not buckle or bend.

If you are worried about the appearance of the columns in the center of your container, many contractors can install small wall segments around them. This gives the building a more welcoming look while also providing more space for insulation materials.

Tips on buying a pre-owned house

If you're buying a pre-owned home, make sure you have it inspected for structural and legal issues to prevent any unpleasant surprises later.

Purchasing a pre-owned home can be a wise decision because it provides you with a ready-to-move-in living space in the neighborhood of your choice. But what if, after taking ownership, you discover that the terrace extension is illegal, the documents are falsified, or that repairing the defective electrical wiring will cost you a lot of money? Being cautious is the best way to protect yourself. Here are a few suggestions:

1. Look beyond the new paint

The house's foundation can be severely damaged behind a glitzy exterior. If you're selling your house, you'll want to make sure the paint isn't peeling or the faucets aren't rusted, but there may be more serious issues. Engage an architect to inspect the property, and he will be able to identify potential problems. There's a good chance the house will need a lot of work. Moldy kitchen cabinets, on the other hand, aren't a reason to cross the house off your list. Examine the damage and seek advice from a professional to determine the cost of repair. You should then ask the owner to renegotiate the selling price to get a better offer. However, if there is a major flaw that will cost you a lot of money and time to fix, you can consider other choices.

2. Peep into the property's history

It is not enough to verify that the individual selling the property is the owner. Depending on the age of the property, you must trace the ownership for a minimum of 20 years and a maximum of three generations. Consult a lawyer who will write a property "search report." If the property was transferred fraudulently, say 10 years ago, all subsequent ownerships, including yours, may be nullified.

Check to see whether the owner of the house has the original "conveyance deed," which states that the land is freehold and can be purchased or sold. In addition, the seller is legally obligated to pay all unpaid debts, such as property taxes and ground rent. In addition, the house's price must be in line with the value of the property as fixed by the government. The price may be slightly higher or lower than this figure, but not below it.

A Supreme Court lawyer, Rajiv Gupta, advises prospective buyers to check the district court records for any litigation involving the land. "If it's an apartment, the information will be in the society documents. What you need is a certificate of no objection in your favor. However, when purchasing an individual property, be cautious of the owner's ability to make several selling deeds," he warns.

If the property was inherited, conduct rigorous legal scrutiny. The best way to avoid a future court dispute is to publicize your planned purchase in a local newspaper and invite any potential claimants to the property.

3. Prepare to spend more

Banks can lend you money to purchase a home, even though it is already owned. They get the property appraised and pay up to 85% of the appraised value or the agreed price, whichever is less. However, they have the right to decline a home loan for a property that is more than ten years old. For example, the State Bank of India does not lend money to people who live in houses that are more than 25 years old.

The only snag you could run into is if the seller decides to under-report the selling price. If you accept, you will be able to pay the additional funds not reported to the bank. But the expenses don't stop there. After you've purchased the home, you'll most likely want to renovate it to your taste. The cost of the renovation may include new woodwork, re-tiling, or lamp fixtures. Remember to add 10% to your cost estimates because you will want to make more changes after you move in than you expected.

4. Check for fees, prospects

Before you sign on the dotted line, find out about any maintenance or parking fees that you might need to pay to the society in your area. A home, whether new or used, will most likely be your largest investment. As a result, it's a good idea and talks to real estate agents to see how much the property will be worth in 10 years. You may be fairly certain that the land would appreciate over time if it is individual property. Unfortunately, this is not true of apartments.

Find out if there are any ways to add value to the property that might increase its value in the future. Any potential for expansion in a self-contained home is a bonus. Check with the right authority to see whether you can let out your apartment to generate income.

CONCLUSION

Building with shipping containers is still a relatively new architecture and construction method, but the trend is still strong.

The development of a container home for shipping can be one of your most satisfying experiences. The cost-saving and mobility are some of the main benefits of building your home using shipping containers. They can also be constructed at incredible speed. They are not only cheap and easy to install but also environmentally friendly; we save about 3500KG of steel for every shipping container cycled up.

However, the prospective thinkers celebrate. Homeowners have also used containers to build a house without ending up with thousands of dollars of debt. The shop owners and some mobile utilities as well as low-income housing developers have also joined the party.

Shipping containers definitely have a place in the world of construction and architecture, but their inherent flaws and restrictions cannot be overlooked. With more experience and time, construction problems will be more effectively addressed and the trend in cargo technology will continue to grow.

Just as in the case of traditional housing, it is important you have the right amount of knowledge and information before you build a container.

Printed in Great Britain
by Amazon